HAIR

Please visit our web site at: **www.garethstevens.com**
For a free color catalog describing Gareth Stevens Publishing's list of high-quality books and multimedia programs, call 1-800-542-2595 or fax your request to (414) 332-3567.

Library of Congress Cataloging-in-Publication Data

Whittaker, Nicola.
    [Creature hair]
    Hair / by Nicola Whittaker.
       p. cm. — (Creature features)
    Includes index.
    Summary: Simple text and photographs show different kinds of animal
  hair, feathers, and fur. Includes a picture glossary which identifies the
  animals pictured and provides information to help with classification skills.
       ISBN 0-8368-3164-0 (lib. bdg.)
    1. Hair—Juvenile literature. [1. Hair. 2. Fur. 3. Feathers.] I. Title.
  QL942.W48   2002
  599.147—dc21   2002019526

This North American edition first published in 2002 by
Gareth Stevens Publishing
A World Almanac Education Group Company
330 West Olive Street, Suite 100
Milwaukee, Wisconsin 53212 USA

This U.S. edition © 2002 by Gareth Stevens, Inc. Original edition © 2001 by Franklin Watts.
First published in 2001 by Franklin Watts, 96 Leonard Street, London WC2A 4XD, England.

Franklin Watts editor: Samantha Armstrong
Franklin Watts designer: Jason Anscomb
Science consultant: Dr. Jim Flegg

Gareth Stevens editor: Dorothy L. Gibbs
Cover design: Tammy Gruenewald

Picture credits:
Bruce Coleman, Inc.: 12.
Images Colour Library: 18-19 (Thomas Kitchin).
NHPA: 4 (Rod Planck), 5 (Laurie Campbell), 6 (Anthony Bannister), 7 (E. A. Janes),
11 and cover (E. A. Janes), 13 and cover (Andy Rouse), 15 (Rod Planck), 20-21 (A.N.T.),
23 (Haroldo Palo, Jr.).
Oxford Scientific Films: 22 (Gerard Lacz).
Planet Earth Pictures: cover-top right (Mary Clay), 8-9 (P. Ravaux), 14 (Mary Clay),
16-17 (M. and C. Denis-Huot).
Still Pictures: 24-25 (Thomas D. Mangelson).
Franklin Watts Photo Library: 26-27.

Printed in Hong Kong

1 2 3 4 5 6 7 8 9 06 05 04 03 02

HAIR

Written by
Nicola Whittaker

Gareth Stevens Publishing
A WORLD ALMANAC EDUCATION GROUP COMPANY

Different creatures

have different **hair**.

Some have **bristles**.

Some have **prickles**.

Some hair is
silky.

Some hair
tickles!

Some hair can **hide**.

Some hair is **bold**.

Some hair

keeps out

water.

14

Some hair keeps out **cold**.

Some hair is

stripy.

Some hair has

spots.

19

20

Some creatures have **no hair**.

Some creatures have **lots**!

Some have **feathers**.

Some have **fur**.

But **my** kind
of hair

is the hair ▌ prefer!

Featured

Macaroni Penguin
Bird (penguin family)
Lives: Antarctic islands
Eats: small water creatures
Has layers of oily feathers
that form a waterproof coat.

Highland Cow
Mammal (cattle/antelope family)
Lives: worldwide
Eats: grass and other plants
Long hair protects it from cold
and snow in winter.

Warthog
Mammal (pig family)
Lives: African plains
Eats: mostly grass and roots
Lets birds eat tiny pests that
live on its skin.

Hedgehog
Mammal (hedgehog family)
Lives: Europe
Eats: worms and insects
Rolls up into a prickly ball to
protect itself when attacked.

Creatures

Weddell Seal
Mammal (seal family)
Lives: Antarctic
Eats: fish and squid
Has a thick layer of fat under its skin to keep it warm.

Emperor Tamarin
Mammal (monkey family)
Lives: South American forests
Eats: fruit, tree sap, and insects
Jumps like an acrobat from tree to tree and runs along branches.

Raccoon
Mammal (raccoon family)
Lives: North America
Eats: almost anything
Uses humanlike paws to handle food and to climb.

Tiger
Mammal (cat family)
Lives: India
Eats: meat
Likes to cool off in water and is a strong swimmer.

Featured

Mallard
Bird (duck/goose family)
Lives: lakes and ponds
Eats: plants and seeds
Male uses its bright feathers
to attract females.

Desert Cottontail Rabbit
Mammal (hare/rabbit family)
Lives: North American deserts
Eats: plants
Uses its white tail to warn other
cottontails when danger is near.

Zebra
Mammal (horse family)
Lives: African plains
Eats: grass
Each has its own unique
pattern of stripes.

Giraffe
Mammal (giraffe family)
Lives: African plains
Eats: leaves
Has unique markings, and its
color gets darker as it gets older.

Creatures

Red-Eyed Tree Frog
Amphibian (frog family)
Lives: Australia
Eats: insects
Its suckerlike toes grip leaves and branches to help it climb.

Puli
Mammal (dog family)
Lives: worldwide
Eats: pet foods
Bred thousands of years ago to herd and protect sheep.

Royal Flycatcher
Bird (flycatcher family)
Lives: South America
Eats: insects
Called "royal" because of its colorful crown of feathers.

Polar Bear
Mammal (bear family)
Lives: northern polar regions
Eats: seals, fish, and birds
The skin under its thick, wooly fur is black.

Index

(**Boldface** entries indicate pictures.)